CORNERSTONES
OF FRE

D0428200

The GREAT RECESSION

BY ANN HEINRICHS

CHILDREN'S PRESS®
An Imprint of Scholastic Inc.
New York Toronto London Auckland Sydney
Mexico City New Delhi Hong Kong
Danbury, Connecticut

Content Consultant
Paul S. Willen, PhD
Senior Economist and Policy Advisor
Research Department
Federal Reserve Bank of Boston
Boston, Massachusetts

Library of Congress Cataloging-in-Publication Data

Heinrichs, Ann.
  The great recession/by Ann Heinrichs.
    p. cm.—(Cornerstones of freedom)
  Includes bibliographical references and index.
  ISBN-13: 978-0-531-25035-8 (lib. bdg.)   ISBN-10: 0-531-25035-0 (lib. bdg.)
  ISBN-13: 978-0-531-26560-4 (pbk.)   ISBN-10: 0-531-26560-9 (pbk.)
  1. Financial crises—United States—History—21st century—Juvenile
literature. 2. Recessions—United States—History—21st
century—Juvenile literature. 3. Financial institutions—United
States—History—21st century—Juvenile literature. 4. United
States—Economic policy—2001–2009—Juvenile literature. I. Title.
  HB3743.H45 2011
  330.973'0931—dc22   2011010824

1 2 3 4 5 6 7 8 9 10 R 21 20 19 18 17 16 15 14 13 12

Photographs © 2012: age fotostock/Norma Jean Gargasz: back cover; Ann
Heinrichs: 64; AP Images: 29 (Mary Altaffer), 48 (Charles Rex Arbogast), 5
top, 14 (Tony Avelar), 4 bottom, 45 (J Pat Carter), 7 (Phil Coale), 32 (Charles
Dharapak), 5 top, 15, 58 (Kevork Djansezian), 2, 3, 8 (Damian Dovarganes),
23 top, 23 bottom, 27 (Richard Drew), 30 (Michael Dwyer), 24 (Hillery
Smith Garrison), cover (Eric Gay), 20 (Mike Groll), 47 (Jason R. Henske), 46
(Nathan K. Martin), 55 (Jacquelyn Martin), 34 (Pablo Martinez Monsivais),
35 (David Pellerin), 40 (Douglas C. Pizac), 38 (Ed Reinke), 37 (Amy
Sancetta), 36, 43 (Paul Sancya), 26 (Reed Saxon), 28 (Sang Tan), 25 (Seth
Wenig), 11; CBS News Archives: 49, 50; Colin Robertson: 54; Department
of Defense/DefenseImagery.mil: 56 top; FEMA News Photo/Michael
Raphael: 44, 59; Getty Images/Mario Tama: 21; Library of Congress: 4 top,
10 (Dorothea Lange), 51 (David Martin); Media Bakery: 18 (Keith Brofsky),
22 (Rob Crandall), 13, 17 (Ariel Skelley): 6; NEWSCOM/John Dooley/Sipa
Press: 16; ShutterStock, Inc./Mark Anderson: 42; Superstock, Inc.: 12; U.S.
Department of the Treasury: 56 bottom, 57.

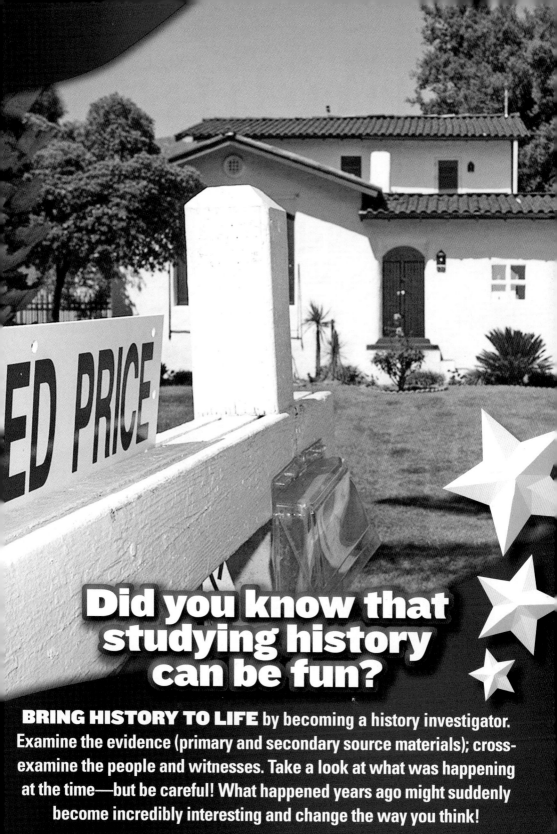

Did you know that studying history can be fun?

BRING HISTORY TO LIFE by becoming a history investigator. Examine the evidence (primary and secondary source materials); cross-examine the people and witnesses. Take a look at what was happening at the time—but be careful! What happened years ago might suddenly become incredibly interesting and change the way you think!

Contents

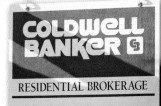

All about Recessions

The Great Recession forced many businesses to close.

In 2007, an **economic** crisis called the Great Recession shook the United States from top to bottom, from the largest corporations down to ordinary families.

Millions of people lose their jobs during a recession. Stores sell fewer goods because people cannot afford to buy them. Prices on goods then either go down or rise too slowly for businesses to make enough money. As a result, factories make

MORE THAN 7 MILLION JOBS WERE

fewer goods and lay off employees to cut costs. Many stores and factories are driven out of business, creating even more unemployment.

The United States has suffered many recessions in the past. The worst recession in U.S. history was the Great Depression, which lasted from 1929 to 1939. The 2007 Great Recession is the worst recession the United States has experienced since then.

Unemployed people were forced to search desperately for new jobs.

LOST DURING THE GREAT RECESSION.

CHAPTER 1

THE HOUSING BUBBLE

Many experts believe the housing bubble was an important cause of the Great Recession.

WHEN YOU BLOW A BUBBLE with bubble gum, it grows bigger and bigger the longer you blow. Eventually, it grows as big as it can get. It bursts and collapses. This is what happened to housing prices in the early 2000s. Prices soared higher and higher during what is known as the housing bubble. In mid-2006, the bubble burst, and the price of homes began to drop. **Economists** consider this housing bubble a major factor in the Great Recession.

People traveled across the country in search of work during the Great Depression.

The American Dream

In the early 1900s, fewer than half of American families owned their homes. Some people rented their homes from landlords. Others lived with relatives until they could afford to buy their own places. For many Americans, home ownership was the American Dream. It meant having control over their own lives. If they owned their homes, no landlord could ever throw them out on the streets.

During the Great Depression, millions of Americans lost their jobs. As a result, they were unable to make their house payments. A quarter of a million families lost their homes during the Great Depression. At that time, lenders often gave borrowers as little as two or three years to pay back their loans. By the end of the 1930s, home ownership in the United States had dropped to 43.6 percent, the lowest level in the 20th century.

Helping Homeowners

Under President Herbert Hoover, Congress passed the Federal Home Loan Bank Act of 1932. The act was designed to make it easier for people to get loans and hang on to their homes. It was the first time the U.S. government involved itself in helping homeowners. Hardly anyone took advantage of the new act, but it paved the way for more effective laws. Franklin D. Roosevelt became president in 1933. He instituted sweeping measures to get the economy back on its feet. He called these programs the New Deal.

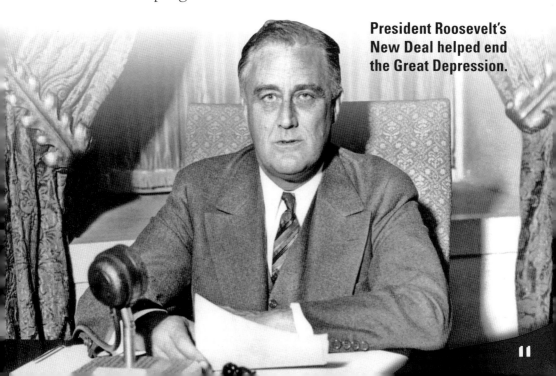

President Roosevelt's New Deal helped end the Great Depression.

The 1933 Homeowners Refinancing Act provided assistance to people who had difficulty paying off their **mortgage** loans. The National Housing Act of 1934 put many people to work building houses. It also got rid of short-term mortgage loans, which required high monthly payments. Borrowers could now stretch out their house payments over many years. The government also promised to protect lenders from losing the money they loaned.

After World War II (1939–1945), the nation enjoyed a booming economy. Many new homes were built, and borrowers had an easier time obtaining mortgage loans. By 1960, more than 60 percent of U.S. families owned their own homes.

Countless new homes were built after World War II.

At the height of the housing boom, most American families owned homes.

The Bubble Grows

Prices naturally tend to rise over time. In 1997, a pound of apples cost about 91 cents. By 2006, that same pound of apples cost about 96 cents, an increase of about 5 percent. Housing prices also rose during that period, but much faster than apple prices did. From 1997 to 2006, the average price of a home increased by 24 percent. That means a house that cost $100,000 in 1997 was worth $124,000 in 2006. Record numbers of people were buying homes. Close to 69 percent of U.S. families owned homes in 2006.

Loans made it easy for almost anyone to purchase a home.

Why did home prices rise so much? And why were more people buying houses than ever before? The answers to these questions are related to one another. For one thing, the **interest** rate on mortgage loans was very low in the late 1990s and early 2000s. If interest rates are lower, then monthly mortgage payments are lower when borrowing the same amount of money. Because of low interest rates, many more people could afford to buy homes.

Most buyers planned to live in the houses they bought. However, others saw the rise in prices as a way to make money. They bought houses and waited for prices to go up even more. Then they sold the houses for profit. With so many people trying to buy houses, sellers were able to charge higher prices. Prices kept rising, and people kept buying.

The Bubble Bursts

Before giving loans, banks and other lenders want to know that borrowers will be able to make their payments. To find out, they look at the borrowers' financial condition, including their employment situation, their annual income, and how much money they owe other lenders. They also check to see if borrowers have good records of making payments on other loans and that they don't already owe too much money. Mortgage lenders also expect borrowers to make **down payments**.

Many lenders were eager to give out mortgage loans in the late 1990s. The buyers' monthly

Predatory Lending and ARMs

Some lenders were guilty of a practice called predatory lending. These lenders approached the loan process like an animal stalking its prey. A company called Countrywide Financial advertised mortgage loans with interest rates as low as 1 percent. Naturally, borrowers flocked to these low-interest loans. However, the fine print in the loan contract revealed that the borrowers were signing up for adjustable-rate mortgages (ARMs). ARMs are different than loans with fixed interest rates. With fixed interest rate loans, the rate never changes, and borrowers pay the same mortgage amount every month. With ARMs, the interest rate can increase over time, which means monthly payments can increase. The interest rate on some ARM loans rose above 10 percent. Some homeowners were unprepared for this. After moving into their new homes, many were unable to afford their monthly payments.

Some companies offered larger loans than what was available elsewhere. But these loans had higher interest rates.

payments gave the lenders a steady stream of income. However, some people who wanted loans fell short of the standards. Some buyers had low-paying jobs or no job at all. Others had several other loans to pay off or could not afford to make down payments. Many banks decided to overlook these problems and issue mortgage loans anyway. These are called **subprime mortgage loans**.

A FIRSTHAND LOOK AT "ZIPPY CHEATS & TRICKS"

In 2008, Mark Friesen, a reporter for the *Oregonian*, a newspaper in Portland, wrote a news story that shocked the country. He reported on an e-mail memo issued by JPMorgan Chase, a leading mortgage lender. The memo, titled "Zippy Cheats & Tricks," provided hints and tips for getting loans approved. Dishonest practices like those in the memo contributed to the housing bubble. See page 60 for a link to read Friesen's article online.

Many families faced foreclosure once the economy began to fail.

Around the country, people began to have trouble paying their mortgages, and more homes were put up for sale. Housing prices dropped, and newly built homes sat vacant. People who had purchased homes at the peak of the market found that their homes were now worth much less than what they had paid. They were stuck with high house payments and no way to sell their homes without losing huge amounts of money.

With loans they could not afford, thousands of homeowners went into **default**. In those cases, the banks began a legal process called **foreclosure**. By the end of 2005, there were 846,982 homes in foreclosure. The housing bubble had burst, and the American Dream had become a nightmare.

CHAPTER 2

THE FINANCIAL CRISIS

Many people use banks for savings and investments.

SUPPOSE YOU HAVE $100, AND you keep it in your dresser drawer for three years. At the end of the three years, you will still have $100. You would have been wiser to put that $100 in the bank. Then it would have been safe, and it would also have grown. The bank would have paid you interest every year. After three years, your $100 might have grown to $110, $115, or more.

People and companies nationwide **invest** their money this way. However, this system collapsed during the Great Recession. Billions of dollars' worth of investors' money was no longer safe, and it no longer grew. In fact, the money they invested began to disappear.

Food pantries helped feed struggling families during the recession.

The Giant Pool of Money

Strangely, the financial crisis began at a time when many people had saved an incredible amount of money. In May 2008, the radio show *This American Life* broadcast an episode called "The Giant Pool of Money." It explained how the financial crisis came about. According to business reporter Adam Davidson, "There's this huge pool of money out there, which is basically all the money the world is saving now."

Both ordinary people and large companies want to invest their savings. Companies have pension plans, or

A FIRSTHAND LOOK AT
DAMON RICH

Artist Damon Rich created a work of art that showed the housing foreclosure crisis in shocking detail. He took an architectural model of New York City and inserted neon-pink triangles on every city block with three or more foreclosures. "In some way, I hope my exhibitions function as strange educational playgrounds for adults," said Rich. See page 60 for a link to see pictures of Rich's art online.

money saved for their employees' retirement. Churches, museums, and charitable organizations have savings. City and state governments also have money saved.

Damon Rich's artwork included models and photographs to help show the scale of the foreclosure problem.

Investment bankers work to make profits using their customers' money.

Naturally, banks hold large amounts of savings too, and they look for places to invest this money. Between 2000 and 2006, the amount of savings worldwide almost doubled, reaching about $70 trillion. The search for good investments became urgent. Where could this giant pool of money go?

Mortgage-Backed Securities

The giant pool of money created a problem for investment banks. Investment banks are different from the banks in your neighborhood. They buy and sell financial items such as stocks, or shares in a business. Investment banks help people by giving them ways to invest their money.

One way to invest money is to buy **mortgage-backed securities** (MBSs). These are "bundles" of mortgage loans all packaged together. Before the early 2000s, buying an MBS was a fairly safe way to invest money. Most homeowners made their monthly mortgage payments, some for as long as 30 years. The investors' money was safe. Also, because interest is added on to the mortgage, the investors' money grew.

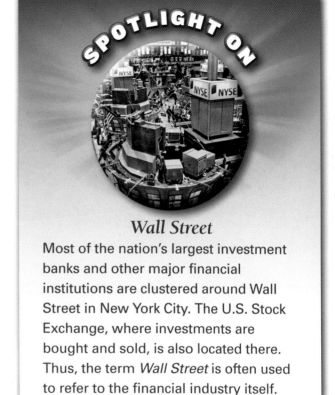

SPOTLIGHT ON

Wall Street

Most of the nation's largest investment banks and other major financial institutions are clustered around Wall Street in New York City. The U.S. Stock Exchange, where investments are bought and sold, is also located there. Thus, the term *Wall Street* is often used to refer to the financial industry itself.

Traders at the stock exchange keep a close eye on stock prices so they can make wise investments.

The Commodity Futures Modernization Act created new opportunities for investment bankers. In 2000, Federal Reserve Chairman Alan Greenspan testified about the act.

With the demand for more investments, investment bankers became nervous. They needed more ways for people to invest their money. They saw that banks were issuing more and more mortgage loans and decided to sell more mortgage-backed securities. Even subprime mortgage loans were bundled together to sell. Investment banks now sold billions of dollars' worth of new mortgage-backed securities.

Investments Gone Wild

Investors who bought these MBSs thought their money would be safe. Many executives in the financial industry agreed. Investors rely on credit rating agencies to find out if an investment is good. Respected agencies such as Moody's rated many of these risky, unstable investments as AAA, the highest possible grade for an investment. Naturally, investors were eager to buy them.

The search for new types of investments continued. Investment companies created financial devices called derivatives that were difficult for investors to understand. Some derivatives are a kind of insurance. They protect investors against losing money. Other derivatives are a way of betting. The investor makes a bet that the value of certain things will go up or down.

Congress made it easy to create and trade derivatives. In December 2000, it passed the Commodity Futures Modernization Act. This law allowed most derivatives to be bought and sold without federal **regulation**. Soon many derivatives were created from subprime mortgage

SPOTLIGHT ON

Warren Buffett

Warren Buffett (1930–) is a billionaire investor, one of the wealthiest people in the world. Buffett, who was born in Omaha, Nebraska, manages an investment company called Berkshire Hathaway. He has pledged to give away 99 percent of his wealth to charity.

Called the Sage of Omaha, Buffett is highly respected in the financial world. In 2003, he called derivatives "financial weapons of mass destruction." He said they were like "time bombs" waiting to go off. Five years later, Buffett's predictions turned out to be correct.

Many people were forced out of their homes after defaulting on mortgage loans.

bundles. Some investment banks even made money betting that their own mortgage-backed securities would decrease in value.

The Crash

It was only a matter of time until this investment system came crashing down. By early 2007, record numbers of homeowners were defaulting on their mortgage loans. Investments based on subprime mortgages had lost much of their value. At the same time, housing prices were plunging. Investments based on the price of homes dropped in value, too.

According to the National Bureau of Economic Research, the Great Recession officially began in December 2007, when the bursting of the housing bubble echoed throughout the financial system. By late 2007, investors would no longer buy mortgage-backed securities. As a result, more than 100 lending companies closed down. Investment banks suddenly had large amounts of MBSs that they could not sell. Other banks

Many politicians promised to change the way banks could use MBSs.

The failure of banks such as Bear Stearns dragged the economy down even farther.

and investment companies that owned MBSs began running out of money.

In March 2008, the investment bank Bear Stearns collapsed. It had been one of the largest investment banks in the country. Another bank, JPMorgan Chase, bought it for a very low price. September 2008 was the low point in the financial crisis. Several more banks and lending companies collapsed. Some were so large and connected that other banks were dragged down with them. Banks around the world collapsed as well, as a result of their unstable U.S. investments.

With less money on hand, the banks that remained in business became very cautious about making loans. But many companies had been getting loans regularly to purchase what they needed to run their businesses. When banks began denying them these loans, some had to lay off workers. Others went out of business. Ordinary people had trouble getting loans to buy cars or washing machines. People stopped spending, and companies stopped growing. The U.S. economy slowed to a crawl.

YESTERDAY'S HEADLINES

The front page headline of the *New York Times* on September 15, 2008—"Lehman Files for **Bankruptcy**; Merrill Is Sold"— reported a major shock to the financial world. "In one of the most dramatic days in Wall Street's history," the article reported, two of the largest U.S. investment banks had failed. The year 2008 was described as a time when "once-proud financial institutions have been brought to their knees as a result of hundreds of billions of dollars in losses because of bad mortgage finance and real estate investments."

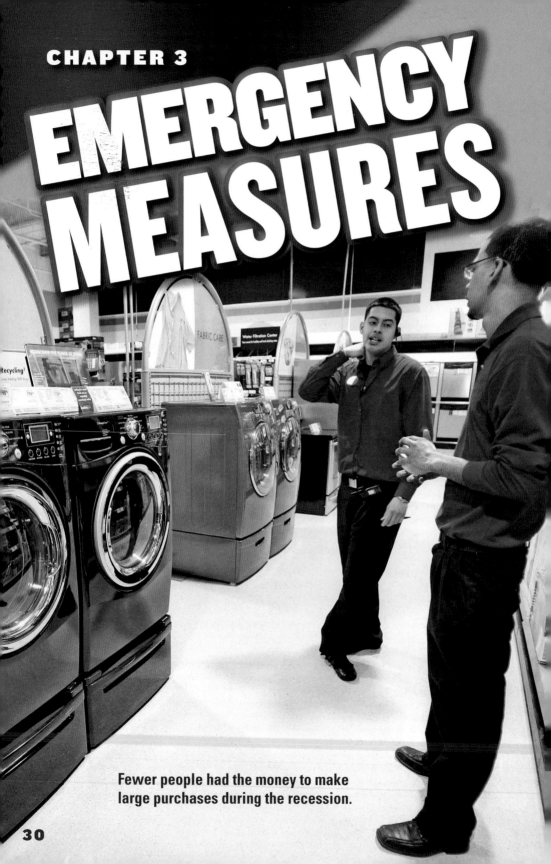

CHAPTER 3

EMERGENCY MEASURES

Fewer people had the money to make large purchases during the recession.

EVEN BEFORE BANKS BEGAN collapsing, the U.S. government had been trying to boost the nation's shaky economy. Throughout 2007, Americans were spending less and less money. This was bad for U.S. businesses. In February 2008, Congress passed the Economic Stimulus Act to get things moving and encourage more spending. The act gave low- and middle-income Americans tax rebates in amounts between $300 and $600. However, the rebates did not have much effect on the economy. Most people used the one-time check to pay bills, make payments on debts, or add to their savings.

President George W. Bush signs the Emergency Economic Stabilization Act.

"Too Big to Fail"

By the end of September 2008, more than a dozen U.S. banks had failed, and hundreds more were teetering on the brink of collapse. The government quickly stepped in to help. Government economists were especially concerned about banks they believed were "too big to fail." These large banks were closely interconnected with other financial institutions and deeply involved in every part of the nation's business activity. Many government officials feared that their failure could bring down the entire U.S. economy.

On October 3, 2008, Congress passed the Emergency Economic Stabilization Act. It was designed to rescue failing banks and other companies devastated by the financial crisis. This kind of rescue effort is often called a **bailout** because it is like bailing, or scooping, water out of a sinking boat.

The act created the Troubled Asset Relief Program (TARP). TARP authorized the U.S. Treasury to buy billions of dollars' worth of mortgage-backed securities from failing banks. This would put money back into those banks and keep them from closing. The secretary of the treasury was put in charge of assigning these funds to various banks. At the time, the secretary was Henry Paulson, a former chairman of the investment bank Goldman Sachs. Paulson had

A VIEW FROM ABROAD

Many Latin American countries lean toward socialism, a system in which goods and services are distributed according to economic needs. Socialism is meant to prevent small numbers of people from controlling large amounts of a country's wealth. Latin Americans were both amused by and scornful of the U.S. bank bailouts. Venezuelan president Hugo Chavez noted, "If the Venezuelan government . . . approves a law to protect consumers, they say, 'Take notice, Chavez is a tyrant!'" He continued, "Comrade Bush is heading toward socialism."

Henry Paulson, treasury secretary under President Bush, worked to end the recession.

been a leader in pushing for the bank bailouts. The TARP program would continue under President Barack Obama. In 2009, Obama appointed Timothy Geithner to head the treasury.

TARP funds were not complete giveaways. Most companies that accepted the assistance agreed to repay the money once they got back on their feet. Many of the nation's largest financial institutions received TARP funds. They included Bank of America, Citigroup, JPMorgan Chase, Goldman Sachs, and Wells Fargo. By 2010, companies that had received TARP funds had paid back more than two-thirds of the money they had received from the government.

The Automobile Industry

The financial industry was not the only business to receive TARP funds. Another recipient was the U.S. automobile industry. During the housing and financial disasters, the automobile industry suffered a crisis of its own. The recession affected the "Big Three" auto manufacturers: General Motors, Chrysler, and Ford. All three are located in or near the city of Detroit, Michigan.

All three companies made cars, sport-utility vehicles (SUVs), and pickup trucks. SUVs and pickups used more fuel than cars consumed. However, they were so popular that the Big Three had shifted much of their manufacturing efforts into making them. As gasoline prices rose higher and higher, sales of these large

Before the recession, the auto industry provided many jobs for Americans.

vehicles dropped. Americans wanted smaller vehicles that could travel farther on less gasoline. People were also increasingly concerned about the environment. Some wanted smaller cars that used less gasoline and created less pollution. Many consumers were looking for vehicles that used alternative fuels such as electricity.

Sales of SUVs and pickups began dropping quickly. Soon, the Big Three were closing down manufacturing plants, laying off workers, closing car dealerships, and offering large discounts to encourage sales. By 2008, the Big Three were on the verge of bankruptcy. Because

Many auto factories were forced to close during the recession.

The Stimulus Bill helped create new jobs but it was unable to completely turn the economy around.

the automobile industry is such an important part of the economy in both Michigan and the nation, the government agreed to help it. Both General Motors and Chrysler received TARP funds, while Ford worked out its financial problems on its own.

The Government Gets Tough

While the bailouts were emergency actions, the government also took measures to improve the U.S. economy for the future. Some measures were designed to create new jobs. Others were introduced to keep a recession from happening again. In February 2009,

TODAY'S PERSPECTIVE

The American Recovery and Reinvestment Act (ARRA) instituted new job-creating projects to help get the economy back on its feet. What are those new projects, and where are they located? How much has been done so far? The Recovery.gov Web site provides an up-to-date interactive map showing ARRA projects across the country. To see the map, go to *www.recovery.gov /Transparency/RecipientReportedData /Pages/RecipientReportedDataMap.aspx*

Congress passed the American Recovery and Reinvestment Act, also known as the Stimulus Bill or the Recovery Act. It provided money for new jobs in transportation, communications, energy, housing, education, scientific research, and many other areas. It also provided tax assistance to struggling businesses and individuals.

Reforming the financial industry was next on the agenda. The poor practices of mortgage lenders and investment bankers had led to the Great Recession. President Obama urged Congress to make reforms so such abuses could never happen again. As a result, Congress passed the Wall Street Reform and Consumer Protection Act in July 2010. It

A FIRSTHAND LOOK AT
THE NATIONAL ARCHIVES

After a president signs a bill into law, the original signed document goes to the Office of the Federal Register in Washington, D.C., to be recorded. Then it goes to the National Archives for permanent preservation. The National Archives also preserves the pen or multiple pens with which the president signed the bill. See page 60 for information on how you can visit the National Archives to see these artifacts for yourself.

was designed to make the United States more financially stable and protect Americans from harmful financial dealings.

This act took a tough stance on financial practices. Among its many provisions, it required U.S. government agencies to oversee the trading of the risky investments that were once unregulated. Much of this supervision would be done by the Federal Reserve, America's central banking system. The reserve is headed by its chairman, Ben Bernanke. The act also included measures to keep banks from becoming "too big to fail." Other provisions were designed to protect citizens from being tricked by lenders. This act has been called the most sweeping reform of the financial industry in many decades. Its purpose was clear. Never again would the financial industry bring the nation to its knees.

CHAPTER 4

REAL PEOPLE, REAL CONSEQUENCES

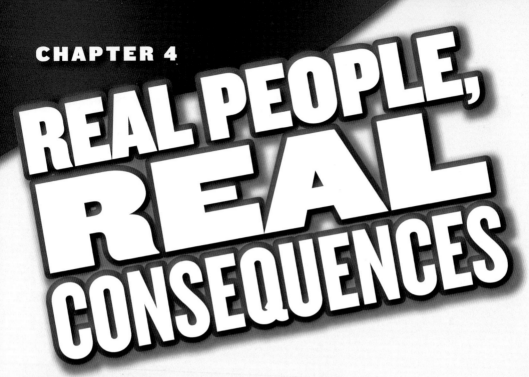

Budget cuts forced public schools to make do with fewer teachers and larger classes of students.

Dance Company

THE GREAT RECESSION WAS

more than a series of bad financial deals. It had real effects on Americans' everyday lives. Lost jobs meant less food on the table. It meant wearing worn-out clothes or driving an unsafe car. Lost homes meant living in inferior housing or moving in with relatives or friends. Loss of savings and investments meant lower standards for education and health care. The effects of the Great Recession rippled throughout the entire economy. It changed the lives of millions of Americans for years to come.

Many Americans bought grocery items in bulk to save on food costs during the recession.

Lifestyle Changes

Many Americans made changes to their lifestyles as the recession took hold. Government figures show that Americans spent less money in 2009 than they had in previous years. It was the first time since 1984 that annual spending dropped. Americans cut back on extras such as entertainment and eating at restaurants. They also spent less on clothing and transportation. People took fewer business trips and vacations. Taking small vacations close to home became a popular trend.

Families had to make difficult choices during the recession. They often did not have enough money to pay for food, medical care, and rent, forcing them to neglect important needs. They put off paying for phone service, electricity, home heating costs, and car repairs. Adding to their emotional stress, many families had to give up their pets because they could no longer afford to buy pet food.

YESTERDAY'S HEADLINES

According to an article in the *New York Times* on July 30, 2008—"Restaurant Chains Close as Diners Reduce Spending"—more and more Americans were choosing to eat at home instead of going to restaurants. The article highlighted the Bennigan's restaurant chain, which had closed that week. Many other restaurants were expected to suffer the same fate.

High Unemployment

For millions of Americans, the worst part of the recession was losing their jobs. According to the U.S. Bureau of Labor Statistics, the average unemployment rate in 2000 was only 4 percent. It rose to 9.3 percent in 2009 and a high of 9.6 percent in 2010. Also, average earnings dropped for workers who still had jobs.

Ordinarily, people who lose their jobs can receive

Unemployed people stand in line to collect their unemployment benefits.

six months' worth of unemployment benefits from the government. This is based on the idea that it takes about six months to find a new job.

During the Great Recession, however, unemployment was much more severe than usual. With so many companies suffering financial trouble or closing, it took unemployed Americans many months, or even years, to find new jobs. In December 2010, Congress voted to extend unemployment benefits for another 13 months. But a great number of Americans were still seeking jobs long after their benefits had run out.

Poverty and Debt

Many families that were just barely getting by slipped into poverty during the Great Recession. According to the U.S. Census Bureau, in 2007, the poverty level in the United States was 12.5 percent, or one out of every eight Americans. It grew to 13.2 percent in 2008 and 14.3 percent in 2009. About one out of every seven Americans—43.6 million people—was living in poverty. It was the nation's highest poverty level since 1994.

One way to measure the financial condition of a household is to compare its debt to its disposable income, or income left after paying taxes. This is the amount of income available for spending or saving.

Formerly employed people were sometimes forced to beg for money.

In 1990, the average household had debts equal to 77 percent of its disposable income. By 2007, the average amount of debt had risen to 136 percent of disposable income. So a family that earned $100,000 a year after taxes had an average of $136,000 worth of debt. The debt includes both credit card debts and mortgages. Since 2007, the debt level has dropped as Americans have adjusted to more affordable lifestyles.

Nonprofit Organizations

The recession was also hard on nonprofit organizations that depend on private donations to operate. These organizations include museums, hospitals, religious groups, and organizations for people with disabilities or

Homeless shelters provided places to sleep for families who lost homes in the recession.

Charity organizations provided food to many people affected by the recession.

special medical problems. Other nonprofit groups help people find jobs, provide the homeless with places to stay, or hold after-school programs for children. Many of these institutions rely on the interest earned on endowments, or large sums of donated money that are invested so they will last for a long time.

During the financial crisis, these organizations found their endowments shrinking to as little as half their former size. Smaller donations went down as well. With less money to spend, people who were usually generous simply could not afford to donate money to charities.

YESTERDAY'S HEADLINES

In June 2009, *New York Times* reporter Steven Greenhouse introduced the term *Generation R*, or Generation Recession. He defined this age group as "the millions of teenagers and twenty-somethings struggling to carve out a future for themselves when the nation's economy is in its worst shape in decades." In his article, titled "As Plants Close, Teenagers Focus More on College," Greenhouse interviewed young people in West Carrollton, Ohio, about their tough choices for the future.

These organizations did what they could to operate with less money. They tried staying open for fewer hours, cutting back on programs and services, and laying off employees. They turned off lights in unused areas to save on electricity costs and did less printing to save on paper costs. Unfortunately, many could no longer afford their expenses and were forced to close.

Generation R

Children growing up during the recession have been called Generation R, meaning Generation Recession. They share their parents' worries about money and jobs. In some cases, parents discussed these problems openly with their children. In other cases, the children may only have overheard their parents' conversations. Either way, life during the recession was different than it had been before.

A CBS News town hall meeting helped show how the recession affected people of all ages.

In May 2009, CBS News held a town hall meeting with young people to discuss how the recession affected them. One girl was approaching her eighth-grade graduation. She decided not to ask for a new graduation dress but to look in her closet for an old dress to wear instead. A high school senior said he planned to go to college, but the recession affected his choices. He was now aiming for state- or city-supported colleges instead of more expensive private colleges.

The young people at the CBS News town hall meeting told stories of how the economic trouble affected them.

There are many other reports of the recession's effect on children. Some children had to get used to being hungry. Some gave their own savings to their parents to help pay for food. Some accepted cutbacks in their spending money as well as smaller birthday and holiday

A FIRSTHAND LOOK AT
KIDS SPEAKING OUT
ON THE RECESSION

In 2009, CBS News held a town hall meeting with kids to talk about the recession. Interviewees discussed how the recession was affecting them and their families, and they posed questions to experts. See page 60 for a link to view the discussion online.

gifts. Some parents were forced to support the family with the money they had saved for their children's college educations. Many young people graduating from high school had to change their minds about going to college. They needed to make money working instead of spending money on their education. At the same time, high

Benjamin Franklin's financial advice about saving money remains a valuable lesson today.

school graduates had trouble finding jobs. After all, many people were already looking for employment.

Like adults hit by the recession, children learned the difference between things they wanted and things they actually needed. They learned about spending carefully, putting off nonessential purchases, and saving money for necessities—just as people had during the Great Depression 80 years earlier. The advice of Benjamin Franklin, one of America's founders, still held true: "Spend less than you get."

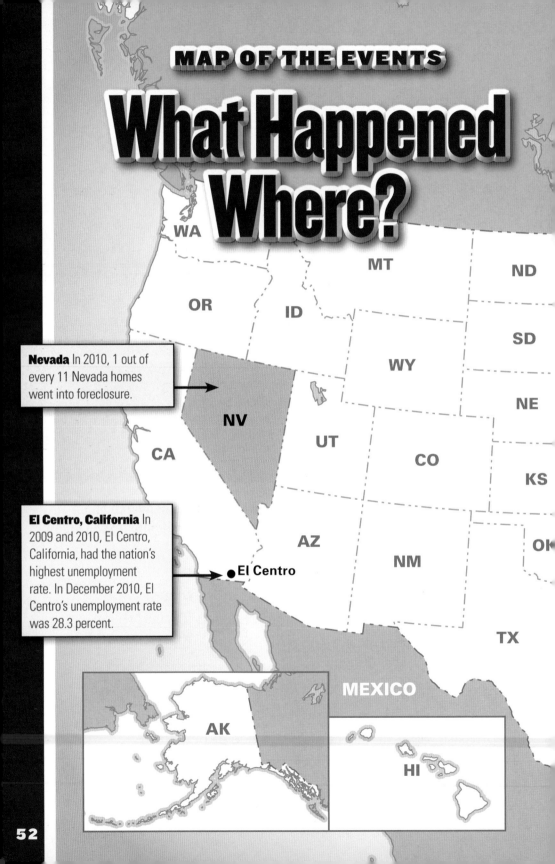

MAP OF THE EVENTS
What Happened Where?

WA

MT

ND

OR

ID

SD

WY

NE

Nevada In 2010, 1 out of every 11 Nevada homes went into foreclosure.

NV

UT

CA

CO

KS

El Centro, California In 2009 and 2010, El Centro, California, had the nation's highest unemployment rate. In December 2010, El Centro's unemployment rate was 28.3 percent.

● El Centro

AZ

NM

OK

TX

MEXICO

AK

HI

Detroit, Michigan The Detroit area is home to the nation's largest car manufacturers: General Motors, Ford, and Chrysler. High fuel prices and lower car sales during the Great Recession brought devastating losses to these companies.

New York, New York New York City is the capital of the U.S. financial industry. The U.S. Stock Exchange and the headquarters of the nation's largest banks are in the Wall Street district. This is where the Great Recession's financial crisis was born.

CANADA

ME

MN

VT NH

WI

NY MA

MI CT

RI

Detroit

IA

PA New York City

NJ

OH Washington, D.C.

IL IN DE

WV MD

MO VA

KY

NC

TN

AR SC

MS AL GA

LA

FL

N

W E

S

0   150   300 mi

0   150   300 km

The New Normal

Foreclosures continue to be a problem for many Americans.

According to the National Bureau of Economic Research, the Great Recession ended in June 2009. The economy hit bottom that month and began its long climb upward. The financial system may have been stabilized, but American life was not. The recovery was long and slow.

It had taken years of financial carelessness to create the conditions that brought about the Great Recession. It would take a long time to repair the damage and build a normal life again.

Even after the economy began growing again in 2009, many people still suffered from unemployment, mortgage foreclosures, and falling home prices. Banks were still reluctant to make loans. Organizations whose savings had shrunk were still adjusting to their loss of wealth. Some economists suggested that America would simply have to get used to a new set of conditions they called the New Normal. With more people practicing careful spending and saving habits and greater financial responsibility, perhaps this New Normal will be the key to full recovery from the Great Recession.

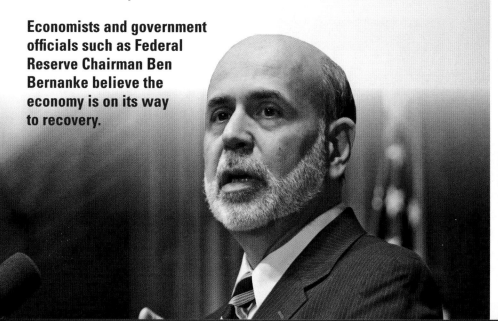

Economists and government officials such as Federal Reserve Chairman Ben Bernanke believe the economy is on its way to recovery.

OFFICIALLY LASTED 18 MONTHS.

George W. Bush

Henry Paulson

Warren Buffett (1930–) is the billionaire manager of the investment company Berkshire Hathaway. He warned against the dangers of investing in derivatives and predicted the financial crisis.

George W. Bush (1946–) was the U.S. president during the Great Recession's housing bubble and financial crisis. He introduced emergency measures such as the 2008 Emergency Economic Stabilization Act and the Troubled Asset Relief Program (TARP).

Henry Paulson (1946–) was the U.S. secretary of the treasury under President Bush and a leader in pushing for bank bailouts under the TARP plan.

Ben Bernanke (1953–) was chairman of the U.S. Federal Reserve during the Great Recession's financial crisis. He oversaw many aspects of the financial industry reform under the 2010 Wall Street Reform and Consumer Protection Act.

Timothy Geithner (1961–) was the U.S. secretary of the treasury under President Obama. He oversaw the distribution of bank bailout funds and the reorganization of the U.S. financial system.

Timothy Geithner

Barack Obama (1961–) was the U.S. president during the aftermath of the Great Recession's housing and financial crashes. He instituted recovery measures such as the 2009 American Recovery and Reinvestment Act and the 2010 Wall Street Reform and Consumer Protection Act.

TIMELINE

2000

December
Congress passes the Commodity Futures Modernization Act.

2006

Almost 69 percent of U.S. families own a home.

July
U.S. housing prices reach their peak; a price decline begins.

2007

More than 100 mortgage lending companies close down; Americans' average household debt reaches 136 percent of their after-tax income.

December
The Great Recession officially begins.

2008

The Big Three automakers are on the verge of bankruptcy.

February
Congress passes the Economic Stimulus Act.

March
The investment bank Bear Stearns collapses.

September
Many large banks and investment companies fail.

October
Congress passes the Emergency Economic Stabilization Act.

2009

Americans spend less money in 2009 than in 2008, the first drop in annual spending since 1984; 14.3 percent of Americans reach the poverty level, the worst poverty rate since 1994.

February
Congress passes the American Recovery and Reinvestment Act.

June
The Great Recession officially ends.

2010

The year's unemployment rate reaches 9.6 percent.

July
Congress passes the Wall Street Reform and Consumer Protection Act.

LIVING HISTORY

Primary sources provide firsthand evidence about a topic. Witnesses to a historical event create primary sources. They include autobiographies, newspaper reports of the time, oral histories, photographs, and memoirs. A secondary source analyzes primary sources, and is one step or more removed from the event. Secondary sources include textbooks, encyclopedias, and commentaries.

The Art of Damon Rich Damon Rich's art project showing foreclosures in New York City helped people see just how bad things had gotten. To see pictures of his project, visit the *New York Times* Web site at *www.nytimes.com/2009/07/08/arts/design/08panorama .html?_r=2&partner=rss&emc=rss*

Kids Speak Out on Recession In 2009, CBS News held a town hall meeting where kids talked about how the recession affected them and their families. To see the discussion, visit the CBS News Web site at *www.cbsnews.com/video/watch/?id=5032497n&tag=related ;photovideo*

National Archives The National Archives in Washington, D.C., houses many of our nation's greatest historical documents. For information on visiting the archives, go to *www.archives.gov/nae/*

"Zippy Cheats & Tricks" To read Mark Friesen's article about the "Zippy Cheats & Tricks" scandal, visit the *Oregonian's* Web site at *www.oregonlive.com/business/index.ssf/2008/03/chase_mortgage _memo_pushes_che.html*

Books

Brezina, Corona. *How Stimulus Plans Work*. New York: Rosen Publishing, 2011.

Cipriano, Jeri. *How Do Mortgages, Loans, and Credit Work?* New York: Crabtree Publishing Co., 2010.

Connolly, Sean. *Banks and Banking*. New York: Franklin Watts, 2011.

Connolly, Sean. *Money and Credit*. New York: Franklin Watts, 2011.

Freedman, Jeri. *The U.S. Auto Industry: American Carmakers and the Economic Crisis*. New York: Rosen Publishing, 2011.

Hollander, Barbara. *Booms, Bubbles, and Busts: The Economic Cycle*. Chicago: Heinemann Library, 2011.

Nagle, Jeanne. *How a Recession Works*. New York: Rosen Publishing, 2010.

Orr, Tamra. *A Kid's Guide to the Economy*. Hockessin, DE: Mitchell Lane Publishers, 2010.

Web Sites

The Generation R Project
www.generation-r.org
Check out information on a project that will document how the recession has affected and will continue to affect Generation R.

This American Life—The Giant Pool of Money
www.thisamericanlife.org/radio-archives/episode/355/the-giant-pool-of-money
Listen to a podcast about how the financial crisis came about.

GLOSSARY

bailout (BALE-out) emergency funds given to businesses to prevent them from collapsing

bankruptcy (BANK-ruhpt-see) a legal declaration of inability to pay debts

default (dee-FAULT) failure to make payments on a debt or loan

down payments (DOWN PAY-munts) partial payments made at the time of purchase on expensive items

economic (e-kuh-NAH-mik) relating to the system of producing, distributing, and consuming goods and services

economists (i-KAH-nuh-mists) experts in the way the economy works

foreclosure (four-KLOH-zhur) the procedure by which a lender takes possession of a house when a homeowner fails to make mortgage payments

interest (IN-trest) a fee that a lender charges for lending money; the borrower pays back both the loan amount and the added interest charge

invest (in-VEST) to use money to buy financial products in order to make a profit

mortgage (MOHR-gij) a loan agreement in which the borrower offers the purchased property as security, or guarantee of repayment to the lender

mortgage-backed securities (MOHR-gij BAKT suh-KYOOR-uh-teez) investments created by gathering together a group of mortgage loans

regulation (reg-yoo-LAY-shuhn) governmental control

subprime mortgage loans (SUHB-prime MOHR-gij LOHNZ) mortgage loans made to people with poor financial conditions or loan histories

INDEX

Page numbers in *italics* indicate illustrations.

ABOUT THE AUTHOR

Ann Heinrichs has a close relationship with the Great Recession. She is the author of more than 230 books for children and young adults on U.S. and world history, geography, culture, and political affairs; science, nature, and ecosystems; and English grammar and usage. However, because of the Great Recession, school libraries and public libraries around the country cut down on book purchases. With a decreased demand for her books, Heinrichs decided to change careers, as many others did during the recession. She went back to school and earned a master's degree in library information science to begin a new career as a librarian. Heinrichs also holds bachelor's and master's degrees in music and has worked as a children's book editor and advertising copywriter. A resident of Chicago, she enjoys bicycling, kayaking, and traveling the world.